AGAINST ALL ODDS

TRILOK S. GULHATI

STARDOM BOOKS

www.StardomBooks.com

STARDOM BOOKS, LLC
112, Bordeaux Ct,
Coppell, TX 75019

FIRST EDITION JULY 2024

STARDOM BOOKS

A Division of Stardom Alliance
112, Bordeaux Ct,
Coppell, TX 75019

www.stardombooks.com
Stardom Books, United States
Stardom Books, India

The author and publishers have made all reasonable efforts to contact copyright holders for permission and apologize for any omissions or errors in the form of credits given. Corrections may be made to future editions.

AGAINST ALL ODDS
Trilok S. Gulhati

p. 126
cm. 13.97 x 21.59

Category:
BIO026000 - Biography & Autobiography:
Personal Memoirs
BUS107000 - Business & Economics:
Personal Success

ISBN: 978-1-957456-27-0

DEDICATION

My parents who inspired me to aim high
AGAINST ALL ODDS.

CONTENTS

ACKNOWLEDGMENTS

I wish to thank my daughter Dr. Soyna who inspired me to write this book. I also wish to thank my publishers Stardom Books India especially two individuals Ms. Ranjitha and Mr. Raam Anand for all their assistance in making my dream come true.

FOREWORD

Mr. Trilok Gulhati, or Trilokji, was a neighbor and dear friend for a decade. When we moved into Prestige Oasis, Ramanji and he were the first to come and welcome us to the community.

Over the years, over a glass or two of wine, I was fortunate to get to know him and his immense achievements in creating and building Sonorome into India's foremost Flavours and Fragrances company; contributing significantly to community development and CSR efforts; in being an active citizen of the neighbourhood; and of being a loving and caring husband, father, and grandfather.

Since I had spent my formative years in Punjab, I felt a special bonding with Trilokji. Through our various conversations over the years, I knew that his family had come from Pakistan during the Partition and had suffered and battled immense hardships.

But it is only after reading this manuscript that I understood the true measure of his achievements: from staying in a refugee-camp, to selling flower-garlands and ice-lollies to help add to the family income, to having to drop out of school—these childhood travails only seem to have strengthened his resolve to succeed. Amidst all the challenges, he ensured he got his under-graduate degree privately and learnt shorthand and typing. His career began as a stenographer at salary of Rs. 104 per month. And from here, he went on to build one of the most respected companies in his sector, with a national and international footprint.

Some things stand out in his story, explaining his remarkable success. First, his ability to make lifelong friends. It is one of these friends who brought his marriage proposal, introducing him to his future wife, Raman Ji and her family; a decisive milestone surely! And these friends also pointed him in the right direction at crucial points in his career. Another key characteristic was having a clear goal and working towards it. He began his private sector career as a stenographer at Hindustan Lever Ltd. But he knew his passion was marketing, and he pursued it, moving within the company and then to different companies with increasing responsibilities. His immense commitment to lifelong learning is also striking; he credits reading TIME magazine with expanding his worldview, and his friends with introducing him to theatre, music, and painting.

His entrepreneurial journey was one of grit and hard work, using his marketing genius to take the Sonorome brand across the country and the world, building a lasting legacy for his family. His commitment to best business practices and environmental responsibility sets an example for all corporates, and his dedication to sharing through CSR and personally should inspire us all.

When Trilokji was alive, we would often discuss the autobiography he was writing. My wife Meena and I offered to look at it and do the last-mile edits to get it ready for publication. Sadly, he left us before he could complete the draft. It is a privilege that Meena could contribute to this after his passing. This documentation of his life's journey is not only important for his family, but also for young people to help them understand how grit, self-belief and hard work can overcome the biggest adversities, and for every entrepreneur on how to tread the hard path to achieve excellence.

It was a privilege knowing you, Trilokji!

V. Raghunathan

A friend of Trilokji

www.vraghunathan.com

THE DAWN THAT NEVER SET

It was a calm day in November, bright and sunny, and my mother had persuaded my father to take me with him. He was going to our village, which was just a few miles away from the city of Mardan (presently in Pakistan) where we lived. I was barely three years old and was excited at the mere thought of an outing. My father had a bicycle. I was to sit on the front bar behind the handle. My mother tied a soft towel on the bar to make it comfortable for me. And this is one of my earliest memories. Sitting on the handlebar of the bicycle, clasping my father's hand, my mind was oblivious to the worries of the world. The picture is so vividly embedded in my mind that I could travel back to that day at any time and become that little kid all over again.

My father's family came from a village called Mayaran, near Mardan in NWFP (North-West Frontier Province). They owned pieces of land, an old house, and some cattle. Since my father had moved to the city, the assets were looked after by my father's uncle and cousins. He used tenants to till the land and shared the produce with them. I was six months old when my parents and my two older siblings moved to Mardan. This change of location was an outcome of circumstantial stipulation. The situation was so grave that the thought of it still sends shivers down my spine.

My grandfather Amir Singh was a landlord and a money-lender. Once, he loaned a large amount of money to a Pathan who defaulted on repayment. My grandfather sought justice at the local civil court, which decided the case in my grandfather's favor. Since the Pathan could not pay, he was sent to jail. When his jail term ended, the Pathan came out filled with fury and rage. While serving the jail term, he had hatched a plan to get revenge.

One day when my grandfather was on a round of his lands on his horse, the Pathan pulled him down and mercilessly murdered him. The horse ran back to the house with the empty saddle, and that was enough for people to figure out what had happened. After this ghastly incident, all our relatives advised my father to leave the village. My mother's family was from the city, and my parents thought we would be safer in Mardan.

However, my father continued to visit the village to meet his uncles and cousins who still lived there and managed the joint family lands. Since the lands belonged jointly to the family, he would occasionally go to claim his share of the crops, etc. It was on one such occasion that I accompanied my father on his bicycle - the ride I remember so vividly.

I attended school in Mardan and was always enthusiastic about going to school, which was in contrast to the attitude of my elder brothers, Harbans and Jaswant, who would frequently play truant. Of the two, Harbans was quite clever and good at studies, whereas Jaswant did not like going to school because he was not good at academics. Our school was a two-storied building. It stood in the middle of a vast compound, which also housed a wholesale Mandi for commodities like sugar, jaggery, and rice.

We lived in a gated property called Nawan (new) Mohalla in Mardan. Our house was a row house consisting of two large rooms, a big verandah, part of which was also the kitchen, and a compound that had bathrooms at its far end. There was no electricity initially, and I remember feeling scared when going to the toilet at night and insisting that someone should hold a lantern while I was there. I remember one such evening when I saw four giant, black poisonous scorpions crawling around in the lavatories in the light of the lantern. Fortunately, we soon got an electric connection, and the compound was brightly lit at night with a big naked electric bulb.

Every day, we walked to the school along with other boys of the Mohalla. My mother's elder sister lived in the same Mohalla, and I regularly interacted with my cousins and aunt. Since my father had limited education and was not trained in any vocation, he did odd jobs, earning a meager salary to support his growing family. Luckily the staple food — wheat and corn — would come from our lands, and there was always enough supply for the whole year.

My mother's family was relatively better off. They had a thriving retail and wholesale business and a big shop in the main Khawaja Bazaar. They lived in an independent house of their own in a better part of the city. My mother's family consisted of my maternal grandparents and their three sons, of whom one was married and had his own family of five children.

They all lived in their double-storied house. I was extremely fond of my maternal grandmother and often spent long hours in that house. I remember walking from our house to my grandparents' home all by myself.

Once, when I was about five years old, I walked away from home and got lost. I do not remember where I intended to go, but I ended up in a crowded area of the town on a bridge spanning the river. I can still recall the details of the road leading up to the bridge and beyond. I do not remember who it was, but someone who recognized me picked me up and brought me back to my anxious mother's arms.

Our house had no municipal water supply, and we had to draw water from the common well. Once a week or so, generally on Sundays, many families would go to the river and wash their laundry. While the mothers attended to the laundry, the children splashed in the river and enjoyed themselves.

One such day, I was standing in the water while my mother did the laundry. I ventured out into the water and was swept away by the current. The next thing I remember, I was struggling against the strong wind driving me out with the flow of the river water. The other kids screamed, and my mother tried to catch me; however, all her efforts went in vain. I remember being rescued by a hefty Pathan who saw me drowning and pulled me out of the water. A lot of water had entered my lungs, so someone put me face down with my stomach atop an inverted earthen pot, which helped discharge water through my mouth and nose. Luckily, I survived to tell the tale!

Mardan which was part of the North-West Frontier Province, is now Khyber Pakthunwala in Pakistan. It is predominantly populated by Pathans or Pakhtoons. Hindus and Sikhs made up less than three percent of the total population before the partition of the subcontinent. While the local people participated in the freedom struggle and had an outstanding freedom fighter in Khan Abdul Gaffar Khan, also known as the Frontier Gandhi, with 1947 approaching, there was a rising sentiment against non-Muslims.

In 1946, several incidents of Hindu and Sikh massacres took place, and their properties were looted. During that time, my father decided that it was not safe to continue living there. With the imminence of partition, he decided to move the family to the safety of the Indian part of Punjab before things got out of hand. However, he was confident that once the country became independent, things would return to normalcy, and we could come back and reclaim our homes and properties. With this in mind, my family left all their belongings behind, locking up the house and hoping to return. However, that could never happen.

I have no memories of my paternal grandparents. My grandfather of course was murdered which was the reason for our moving to Mardan, but I think my grandmother too died before we moved. However, I have very fond memories of my maternal grandmother and grandfather. My naani was a slim, beautiful, gentle person who never raised her voice. She was extremely fond of me and encouraged me to spend as much time in her house as possible. My grandfather was a businessman, and while he was pretty loving too, being a man of the world, he was fonder of his son's children!

My Mother

WRATH OF PARTITION

We travelled to Patiala from Mardan by train. I do not remember if we changed trains anywhere on that route. I recollect that the train journey was not easy; the family often struggled to find drinking water on the platforms when the train stopped. We were instructed to get water from pots marked 'Hindu Water' and avoid pots marked 'Muslim water.' I did not understand the difference, but my father told me 'We do not eat or drink with Muslims.' During the train journey, food was inadequate, and often at night, the train would run without lights in the compartments.

The news of the exodus of Hindus and Sikh refugees like us had travelled ahead of us, and as we entered Punjab, on the Indian side, there were special 'Langars' (community kitchens) at the platforms, and we were welcomed. We landed in Patiala on a bright and sunny day at the beginning of March 1947. And along with the other passengers, we were taken in a truck to a refugee camp on the outskirts of Patiala, an area known as Dera Baba Jassa Singh.

My family was allotted a tent and given mattresses to sleep on. Breakfast, lunch, and dinner were served in the Langar, where everyone would sit on the floor in a row and we were all served basic food consisting of dal, chapattis, and occasionally one vegetable preparation. Breakfast was tea and one paratha per person.

The authorities had set up a primary school in the camp where all the children were enrolled.

Life in the refugee camp was dull and monotonous but eventually became a routine.

The Maharaja of Patiala held a large gathering (durbar) on Baisakhi day (the 13th of April) for the refugees. It was a grand, regal affair held in the pristine gardens of Moti Mahal. The Maharaja sat on the throne in his royal robes, a jeweled crown, and all the other royal paraphernalia. He was a tall and handsome man and exceptionally well groomed. His royal courtiers and supporters would walk up to him with expensive gifts, bow before him, and seek his blessings. They then would move to their appointed place under the decorated Shamiana.

The general public was not allowed anywhere near the celebration and watched the proceedings from a distance — overawed by the event's grandeur. There was a variety of food for everyone, including a vast array of different sweets. This was a wonderful change from the mediocre fare of the refugee camp. The royal band played music, and soldiers in colorful uniforms marched past. The celebrations ended with a procession in which the Maharaja rode on his elephant, preceded by a band and a troop of armed soldiers marching through the city's main streets.

My father was a very self-respecting man and couldn't live on the charity of others in the refugee camp for too long. He decided to move out earlier than any of our extended family. We rented a portion of a house in the Raghomajra neighborhood in Patiala, and my father began looking for work. I do not remember what kind of work he did, but we children were adequately fed. I was enrolled in a school in town, and so were my two elder brothers.

Life went on and settled into a routine of sorts. I do not remember any significant events of this period except one. One day I along with some children from the neighborhood decided to climb a jamun tree. We plucked a lot of jamuns — some not even ripe enough for eating — and gorged on them. The next day, I had an upset tummy. My mother got very worried about my condition and tried giving me some home remedies. However, I didn't feel any better.

When my father returned from work and was told of my condition, he went out and bought a bottle of whisky. He asked me to have a big spoonful of whisky in the evening, and one more at bedtime. The whisky had a soothing effect on me, and I slept. The following day I was back to normal.

As the news of Partition spread, we heard that Muslims in west Punjab had turned violent — killing men, women, and children of Hindu and Sikh families and looting all the properties. The stories of an entire train loaded with corpses from Pakistan were doing the rounds. That infuriated the Sikhs and Hindus on this side of the border, and they retaliated by attacking, looting, and killing the fleeing Muslim families. After the mass killings, the late monsoons in August and September filled the streets with water. I recollect seeing corpses floating in the water on our roads.

I also heard heart-rending stories of Muslim women asking for mercy and offering to convert to Hinduism or Sikhism. Some of them married the Sikhs or Hindus responsible for saving them in such situations.

With the intervention of the two governments, there was an exchange of Sikh, Hindu, and Muslim women on both sides. This created further trauma for those who had to abandon their newly found families and were forced to return to their country of birth.

"Living is a process of developing oneself. Without experiencing pain from disconcerting periods of our lives, we would be different person, perhaps a lesser person."

–Kilroy J. Oldster
Author

15TH AUGUST, 1947 AND THE DAYS THAT FOLLOWED

When the partition of the country was announced, and millions of people were celebrating the Independence of India, it was a sad day for my family. My father was depressed as he thought of all that he had left behind in what was now Pakistan. The thought that he would never be able to return to his home and lands in Mardan affected him. He retreated into his shell and refused to work. If this had happened in the present times, he would probably be diagnosed with PTSD and given treatment.

Finally, one day he announced that he was going to Delhi (Shahdara) to meet one of his friends who was also a refugee. He disappeared for a while and didn't communicate with us at all. We had no idea of his whereabouts and kept hoping to hear from him. My mother would reassure us that he would soon return home with money. She was a strong woman and took charge of the family.

We were desperately poor, and my mother realized that she had to take some tough calls. She asked my elder brothers to quit school and begin working to bring in some income. They began working odd jobs and did whatever they could to keep the family fed. It was a challenging phase of life. What my older brothers earned was barely enough to feed the family. My younger brother and I also chipped in by doing odd jobs. Sometimes we sold ice lollies and sometimes garlands of flowers that our mother strung together. Life was cruel, and I vividly remember our struggling days. I remember several nights where we slept hungry or were given a biscuit and tea and told to go to bed.

Despite the extreme challenges, my brothers and I managed to keep our spirits high. We did whatever work we could find, and the family survived.

My eldest brother was keen that all his younger brothers should continue their studies. During this time, we were allotted a house from among the homes left by the Muslim families who had moved to Pakistan.

Life improved on another front too. My father returned home, and our family was complete again. He tried his hand at a few small businesses before finally setting up a small flour mill, which soon stabilized and did well.

More than anything else, the partition created several million refugees on either side of the border. It took several years for these refugees to find their bearing in the new environment. While the refugees from northwest Punjab, enterprising and hardworking by their very nature, settled fast, the refugees from east Bengal, who had moved to Calcutta, continued living in refugee hovels until the sixties.

"Anyone who stops learning is old, whether at twenty or eighty. Anyone who keeps learning stays young."

—Henry Ford
Industrialist, Business magnate

EDUCATION IS A LIFELONG PROCESS

After the refugee camp school, my younger brothers and I were enrolled in a free government school. It was, however, a primary school, and since I was already in the fourth standard, I could only study there for one year.

My mother, who understood the importance of education, began the hunt for another school for us that would provide free education. She found a good school and pleaded with the headmaster, a kind man, to enroll me. The headmaster completed the paperwork and asked my mother to sign it and got me a tuition-fee exemption.

This school was only up to Std.8. So, after completing my studies there, I was enrolled in a privately run coaching class that prepared children for the High School Board examination. I had to pay a fee of Rs.10 per month. To pay for my fees and help the family, I began tutoring young children every evening.

The headmaster of my coaching class school was Mr. Dutt, a very passionate and dedicated teacher, and a great patriot. He had lost his right arm in an accident and wrote extensive notes on the blackboard with his left hand. He had studied several versions of Indian history and taught us passionately. He was critical of how the history of India was written by the British authors, who he thought had portrayed Indians and the leaders of pre-British India in a bad light.

I passed my Std.10 (Matriculation Examination) from Punjab University, topping my class of 40 students, and getting high enough grades to be on the merit list. This ensured my admission into Mahendra College, Patiala. I was also fortunate to be considered for the 'Refugee Students Fund Scholarship.' That, in addition to the exemption of total tuition fees, made me feel good since I no longer had to ask my mother for pocket money. I could get some decent clothes for myself with the money I received.

After excelling at school, I found college studies challenging. I had opted for Economics and Mathematics as the main subjects, along with English. I realized that the level of Mathematics in college was very high, and I found it difficult to cope. My grades in internal examinations began dropping, and at the end of the first year, though I had managed to pass my exams, I was anxious about the next few years. I managed to find a senior student who was pursuing a degree in Mathematics to help me. I paid him a small tuition fee from my scholarship money, and he helped me sail through. I cleared my Intermediate exams.

Meanwhile all was not well on the home front. The financial situation was not good, and we barely got by. I then decided to drop out of college and look for work. With no college degree in hand, it was not easy to find a job. So, I decided to enroll myself in typing and shorthand classes. These skills helped me get my first job as a stenographer at Rs.104 per month. A few months later, I got a better job in the Municipal office, and then landed a respectable position in a company at Rs.250 per month. I was hungry for more and kept scouting for better opportunities.

While I enjoyed working, I realized that a college degree was important if I wanted to grow. So, I enrolled myself in a private college where I could attend classes early in the morning and then go to work. Several of my classmates were also in similar situations. Many were married and were responsible for taking care of their families. I was able to finish my B.A. while working and passed with excellent grades. I had taken Hindi as the optional subject in B.A., but there were no classes for it. As the exams neared, I realized that I needed to do well in Hindi to improve my overall marks. I found an old Panditji near my house and started going to him for tuition. He ran me through my only textbook, and I passed in Hindi, securing 23 out of 50 marks. This padded my overall marks.

Around that time, I saw an advertisement in the paper by Hindustan Lever Ltd. (Unilever) looking for a stenographer for their Chandigarh area office.

I applied for the post and was called for an interview. I was interviewed by a brilliant, handsome, and polished young man named Vijay Lamba, who would be my boss for the next two years. He played an important role in my future.

My new job as Mr. Vijay Lamba's assistant was exciting since it allowed me to work independently when he travelled (which was quite often). He relied on me to take care of mails from the eight salespeople who reported to him, correspondence from the Branch office in Delhi, and the occasional mail from the head office in Bombay. Mr. Lamba was happy with my work and found me to be responsible and diligent. He began relying on me, trusted me to handle things independently.

This was the beginning of a new chapter in my life. It transformed my view of the world. Mr. Lamba subscribed to the Time magazine, and this usually arrived when he was away travelling. Initially, out of curiosity, I would glance through the magazine, and as time passed, I started to enjoy reading it. Coming from a lower-middle-class family, I had little knowledge of life outside our small social circle. My vision and understanding of the world were limited by my narrow circumstances. Reading Time magazine for me was in a way, a continuation of my education. I began reading the magazine every month from cover to cover and enjoyed learning about world affairs, the arts, business, and various other topics covered in the magazine. This contributed to my expanded worldview, and I credit regular reading of this one magazine as a huge factor in my growth and progress throughout my life. Till recently, I regularly subscribed to the Time magazine and read its contents thoroughly. I am happy that my children and grandson Agastya have also picked up. this habit from me. In the last 4-5 years I switched from the Time to the Economist as I began noticing that the former was biased against India and third world countries.

"Your time is limited, so don't waste it living someone else's life. Don't be trapped by dogma — which is living with the results of other people's thinking. Don't let the noise of others' opinions drown out your own inner voice. And most important, have the courage to follow your heart and intuition. They somehow already know what you truly want to become. Everything else is secondary."

–Steve Jobs
Co-founder of Apple Inc.

LIFE AS A SALESMAN

During this period, I also began attending sales conferences. I was a people's person and wanted to explore a salesman's life. I realized that I would enjoy it more than a sedentary office job. I then sought my boss Mr. Lamba's advice and asked him if I could be considered for the position of company salesman. He wanted to help me grow, and even at the risk of losing a good assistant, he recommended me when a position opened up. After a series of interviews in Delhi, I was selected as a salesman in the Soaps' Division of Hindustan Lever.

After the initial field training, I was given independent charge of a territory with its headquarters in Bhatinda, Punjab. This was the most backward part of Punjab in the early '60s. The area was also called the 'Wild West of Punjab' for its dubious record in murders, lawlessness, and the lack of an educated population. Bhatinda was a major railway junction, and in the absence of a hotel, many salespeople like me would use the railway retiring rooms as our temporary abode during our travels.

I took my job as a salesman quite seriously and followed all instructions to the tee. As a result, my territory was well organized, and my superiors were quite happy with my progress. I was soon given a chance to work on a mobile sales van with a built-in cinema unit. We would go to tiny towns where there were no local cinemas. We would gather crowds, sell the company's soaps to consumers directly, and invite them for cinema entertainment in the evening. Most 16 mm films we showed were on wildlife and song-and-dance sequences, interspersed with our advertising clips. This was a tremendous experience, and I learned a lot by travelling in areas of rural Punjab, Himachal, and Jammu & Kashmir.

I spent four years in Hindustan Lever, and these were significant years during which the company introduced Surf detergent powder and launched Lux soap in various colors—breaking away from the original 'only white' Lux policy. In a short stint of four years, I worked in urban and rural markets, on a cinema van, and was part of launch conferences for Surf and Lux, and also attended a training program in Bombay at the company's training center 'Gulita' which is now a tower housing senior members of the company staff.

That was my first-ever visit to Bombay, and it opened my eyes to my own country. While attending the training course during my trip to Bombay, I learnt more about company policies, which I found to be at variance with my ambitions. I discovered that the company followed a policy of 'direct recruitment' of management trainees, and the young men like me who came into the company as 'salesmen' had abysmal growth prospects. This for me was disappointing and not in line with what I wanted for my future. I decided that I would not stay with the company for too long. I would move to a smaller company, get into a managerial position and later perhaps, get back into a multi-national company.

Luckily, for me, a job opening came up in Gabriel India, a company where Jack Chadha, the younger brother of a very dear friend, was the sales manager. They wanted a regional representative in Delhi and indicated that it was like a Regional Manager's job. I applied for it, got the job, and moved to Delhi.

"Let there be spaces in your togetherness and let the winds of the heavens dance between you. Love one another but not make a bond of love: Let it be rather a moving sea between the shores of your souls."

–Kahlil Gibran
Writer, Poet, Philosopher

UPS AND DOWNS

When I joined Hindustan Lever in Chandigarh, I happened to befriend the Chadha family. Chadha's (father, three sons) lived in Chandigarh and were the exclusive agents for Usha sewing machines, fans, etc. I became friends with the eldest of the three sons — Daulat Rai. I thoroughly enjoyed his company even though he was almost ten years my senior. We shared common interests in reading and discussing books and drinking beer together! We spent a significant amount of time with each other.

It was Jack Chadha who was instrumental in my leaving Hindustan Lever and joining Gabriel. He was the Sales Manager in Gabriel, Mumbai. They were looking for a regional representative in Delhi to take care of their business in North India. Gabriel did not have their own office in Delhi and used the Firestone Tyre Company as its distributor for Gabriel shock absorbers. I was asked to sit in the Firestone office in Old Delhi and operate from there.

My job was to promote the sales of Gabriel shock absorbers to the replacement market in north India. This meant promoting the product to garages, fleet owners, and motor parts dealers. My efforts were coordinated with Firestone sales staff, who primarily pushed the sales of their tyres but also helped the accessories business I did an excellent job of promoting the brand and creating awareness in the region about the role of a shock absorber in a vehicle's comfort. Firestone staff was delighted with my enthusiasm, and the head of the Firestone office, Mr. Sucha Singh, a tyre industry veteran, met me often. He told me stories about how he pioneered the Firestone brand in India by personally delivering tyres in a horse-drawn carriage (tonga) to truck owners. So much so that Firestone Tyre became known as 'Sucha Singh Tyre.'

To show their gratitude, the Firestone Tyre company invited him to visit the head office in Akron, Ohio. To show appreciation for the excellent work Sucha Singh had done, half a dozen senior managers of Firestone showed up at the airport wearing turbans to honor the Sikh man!

Based on my excellent work, I was promoted and brought to Bombay to help with the floundering business of Victor Gaskets——a company promoted by Gabriel founders. Encouraged by their good experience with Firestone, the management had made exclusive selling arrangements for Victor Gaskets with another tyre company, Goodyear. Goodyear, however, did not take that business seriously, and the product didn't show signs of succeeding. I tried for a while to fix things but soon realized that Goodyear was not putting enough effort into establishing the Victor brand, which was a tiny part of their overall business.

I advised the company to break up with Goodyear and set up its own marketing network. This was a very dramatic suggestion and rattled everyone for a while. However, I presented them with details of my plan for setting up a national network of dealers who would market our product, and the project was approved. The task of breaking up with Goodyear and setting up an alternative network was thrown at me as a challenge.

I travelled to Calcutta, checked into the Grand Oberoi, and telephoned the Managing Director of Goodyear, an American who was twice my age, and introduced myself. I briefly explained to him that we were not happy with how things were going and that I was in Calcutta to terminate the relationship with their company. It was clear from his response that he did not take me seriously. He said he would call me back. He telephoned my company's Managing Director to check on my statement's veracity. In the meantime, I telephoned Mr. Anand, my boss, and updated him on my telephonic conversation with the gentleman. Mr. Anand told the M.D. of Goodyear that I was in Calcutta on his behalf and had the mandate of the company to negotiate with Goodyear.

By the following day, the situation had changed. Goodyear sent a car to my hotel to pick me up and take me to their office. I spent the following five days in Calcutta sorting out all issues connected with the break-up and returned to Bombay to a hero's welcome by my company.

The next few months were hard for me — traveling extensively and appointing dealers to sell our gaskets; taking care of quality problems; handling the return of unsold stock; and reconciling the accounts with Goodyear. Even though I left the company later on a matter of principle, I have always felt proud of how I handled that assignment, especially how I dealt with the American boss at Goodyear.

Later, I left Gabriel/Victor in a huff and was suddenly without work in a big city like Bombay, where I had no friends or family. I kept the news of this to myself, not letting my family know.

I was confident that I would find another job soon and planned to announce it to my family only then. My self-confidence started to wane as I entered the second week of unemployment. Luckily, I met Mr. Jerry Swatek, Managing Director of Siemens India, at the home of a friend of mine. My friend introduced me to Jerry and praised me for my work at Gabriel. Jerry said his company was looking for someone with my experience and said he would get back to me.

The next day, the Personnel Manager of Siemens telephoned me and said Mr. Swatek had asked him to call me for an interview. I got the offer from Siemens and was made

Assistant Manager for the SPT (Sales Promotion and Training) department, headed by Mr. S P Mathur, a senior Technical Manager at Siemens. I accepted the job without realizing that Siemens was a highly technical company with a very peculiar set-up of technical and commercial managers running each department.

Their technical managers were outstanding, experienced engineers who understood the technical side of the customer's business. In contrast, the commercial managers were people who understood commercial aspects like sales tax, import duties, contract law, etc.

There was no concept of 'Marketing' as I understood it based on my stint at a consumer products company and later selling to traders. I was however content with having an excellent job located a comfortable distance from my residence and decided to stay in the position. I enjoyed the company of my colleagues and forged some lasting friendships — Mahesh, Sigrid Agarwal, Ranbir, and Baljeet Sachdeva. I was impressed by the H.R. policies of Siemens, which were based on respect for professional managers.

I got a glimpse of this when I decided to leave Siemens. I was called by Dr. Baer, the Managing Director, who asked why I was leaving. He told me that there was a policy in Siemens that whenever a manager leaves, the head of the business in that country was supposed to send a brief report to world headquarters explaining why the manager had decided to exit. I was very impressed and left the company on a very cordial note and am still in touch with many people there.

"Don't get distracted. Never tell yourself that you need to be the biggest brand in the whole world. Start by working on what you need at the present moment and then what you need to do tomorrow. So, set yourself manageable targets."

–Jas Bagniewski
Co-Founder of Eve Sleep

HOMECOMING TO FMCG

It happened that while I was working with Siemens, I saw an ad in the newspaper by Warner Hindustan (Warner-Lambert) asking for an 'All India Sales Manager' for their consumer products division. This company was based in Hyderabad. I applied for it and was interviewed by Mr. S L Rao at the Taj Mahal hotel in Mumbai. This was a shortlisting exercise in which I did well. A few days later, the company's Personnel Manager, Mr. Surinder Singh (a perfect gentleman), called me and asked me if I could travel to Hyderabad for a day for the next round of interviews.

They sent me an air ticket, and I was asked to travel on a Sunday to meet with them in Hyderabad. Mr. Surinder Singh picked me up from the airport and drove me to Secunderabad Club for an interview with the Managing Director, Mr. N H Israni. After I shook hands with him and sat down, he asked me what I would like to drink. I chose a gin and lime, and we started talking. I soon realized this was no social call, and this man was grilling me. His technique was to drive one to the brink and hope the guy would break. He asked me many questions starting with my life as a salesman in Levers, to my ambitions etc. After an hour or so of grilling, I was let off - I was very stressed but was very confident of the way I had handled the conversation.

Mr. Surinder Singh drove me to a hotel (Percy's Hotel — it no longer exists) where they had booked a room for me. He then went into salary negotiations. After that, he left me to relax, promising to come back and drop me at the airport.

I returned to Bombay quite pleased with myself. My formal appointment letter arrived in a couple of days, and I submitted my resignation to Siemens.

I had been married for a few years by then and was the proud father of a lovely little girl. We started preparing to leave

Mumbai and set up a home in Hyderabad. We drove to Hyderabad, having sent our household items by truck. I had a small car, Standard Herald. My wife, daughter Soyna who was then one-plus, and I left on our drive. We reached Pune and spent the night there. The next day we drove to Hyderabad. It was scorching hot, and our little daughter got so tired of being in the car that even later in Hyderabad, she would not get into the car for days. We were booked into a small hotel in the Abids area of Hyderabad and started looking for a house.

We found one in Eramanzil in the Panjagutta area and settled in. We found help in the form of an old Muslim lady called Amma by us, who was a great support with Soyna.

I started my job in right earnest. My Director, Surendra Rao, told me I was to run a training program for inducting the first bunch of salesmen who were joining in a week. He then took me to meet the M.D. Mr. Israni said that I should prepare a manual for sales reps, and when I told him I did not know enough about the company to be able to write a manual, his reply was short - this would be the best way to learn!

My work schedule was punishing — I would leave home at 0730 am and return when dinner was on the table. In addition, I was traveling 15-18 days a month, leaving no time for the family or my lovely daughter. But like all career-oriented young, ambitious managers, I took to the job like a crazy workaholic and was bent upon making a success of the challenge before me.

"If you are working on a product that's going to be consumer-facing, then feedback is invaluable. You should be out there being brave and talking to people and asking for feedback as much as possible."

–Emily Brooke
Co-founder of Blaze

LAUNCH OF CHICLETS & HALLS MENTHOLYPTUS IN INDIA

Even before Warner launched any product in India, I was asked to set up a network of authorized dealers in all principal cities and towns of India — approximately 150. This was not easy since we had no product to show to potential dealers, nor did we have any format for a dealership. Imagine asking a trader to commit to being a dealer without seeing or knowing the product they would deal with!

The only information we gave to potential dealers was that they would be dealing with an international brand like Chiclets, and the company would provide all marketing support in the form of advertising. The sheer size of the country and the challenge of appointing more than 100 stockists was something that had me running like a madman. I was traveling 20 or more days a month, crisscrossing the country, and creating a network before the actual launch of the product. This was physically exhausting and took a toll on my family life. My young wife was suddenly a single parent to our young daughter in a city where she was new and didn't know many people.

My wife, with practically no help from me, full credit to her, managed the situation very well, coping with minor accidents and injuries to the child while I was away. Even when I was at Hyderabad, I would leave for work at 8 am and never return before dinner. I was so exhausted then that I would go to bed immediately after dinner.

Anyway, Chiclets was launched, and my team did a great job of distributing the product widely. We not only sold to the usual confectionery outlets, but also to cinema canteens and many other unconventional outlets like barber shops, etc. In a big metropolis like Bombay, my target was that one should not be able to walk more than 50 yards without seeing a Chiclets outlet. In a way, we created history in India's marketing and distribution world. Some students in management schools wrote papers on the success of Chiclets.

The management rewarded me by sending me on a trip to Thailand and Hong Kong. Thailand has traditionally been a big candy market, and the company's idea was to expose me to how business was run there.

They were also keen that I study the marketing and distribution of another of their products, Halls Mentholyptus, a cough drop, in the category of adult candy, before the product was launched in India. Diethelem was the company that handled the distribution for Warner-Lambert in Thailand (and in some other countries), and they were my hosts in Thailand.

And oh boy, what hospitality they offered! I was taken to the best places for lunch and dinner almost daily. They deputed a gentleman called Khun Suwan as my guide. Khun Suwan took me on trips outside Bangkok to places like Chinghai, Chengrai, Prachuab, etc., where we worked with the company's salespeople as they sold Halls and Chiclets. This was a fantastic experience. Towards the end of my trip, the management of Diethelm organized a party for me, and what a lavish affair it was! The party was aboard a boat on the river Chao Phya. The boat started from a five-star hotel in Bangkok and sailed almost to the point where the river joined the sea, with a grand festivity of drinks, food, music, and dancing.

I learned a lot from this experience and discovered how low the hospitality standards in India were at that time.

Before I left for Bangkok, my mother-in-law had given me the phone number of one of her friends by the name of Narula. She insisted that I call them up and seek their help if needed. So, like a dutiful son-in-law, I called up Narula Uncle

(Mohinder Singh Narula) and introduced myself. He was extraordinarily gracious and came to meet me in my hotel. He asked me if I needed any help, especially if I needed any local money (in those days, the Reserve Bank of India allowed only 6 Pound Sterling per day and expected the submission of a report with details of expenses!).

When I told him that I had sufficient money, he suggested I buy some gold as the price of gold there was substantially lower there compared to India, and it was of higher purity. I thanked Narula uncle and told him I had no interest in buying gold.

I slowly realized that the Narula's were quite influential. They owned businesses such as a rubber factory, a bowling alley, and a few shopping malls. Mr. Narula took me under his wing, guided me about the places to see in Bangkok, and encouraged me to have a massage, recommending a massage parlor that he thought was 'clean.' He invited me to their home for a meal and took me to a bowling alley.

From Bangkok, I flew to Hong Kong, where I had a meeting at the local office of Warner-Lambert. That trip was primarily for sightseeing and shopping with the bit of money that I had. When I returned to India, I realized how much catching up India had to do. For instance, I was impressed with the automatically opening doors in stores and offices. I hadn't seen that anywhere in India. The other thing which impressed me in Hong Kong was the vending machine. I went to see a movie, and in the movie theatre, there was a vending machine to dispense coffee. What fascinated me was that one could order coffee in different combinations - with sugar, without sugar, with milk, without milk, and all at the press of a button. This, too, was nowhere to be seen in India.

On the whole, that first overseas trip opened my vistas, and I discovered what lay outside India and to what extent India had to progress.

"When in doubt, bootstrap. Using your own personal resources is the easiest way to start a business. You don't have to convince investors about the merits of your idea. You just have to convince yourself."

—Ryan Holmes
Co-founder of Hootsuite

TWO FAMILES TIE THE KNOT

It's time for a flashback to the parallel events in my personal life.

When I turned 25 and had my first executive job in Mumbai, my parents started asking me the inevitable question — when would I get married? Every time I went home to visit my parents, I would face the same question from my mother, and each time I evaded the issue, saying I still had time.

When I was 27 and came home to meet my parents, my mother cornered me and asked the same question again. When I tried to wriggle out of the conversation, she made me sit down and said, "Listen carefully." This kind of stance was very unusual for my mother, so I sat in front of her, and she said, "If you have decided to remain a bachelor all your life, I will never ask you to marry. But if you are unsure, this is the time to consider marriage."

This made me think, and a few months later, when a proposal was brought by my dear friend Daulat Rai Chadha, I thought it was worth a serious thought. I trusted his judgment in these matters, and when he told me about Raman and her family, I said I was open to the suggestion. So, he and his wife Satya Bhabhi, arranged to get Raman and her parents over to Chandigarh for a meeting with my family and me. Raman was still in college in Ludhiana and was a bit young - she was 18, and I was 27. I thought the age gap was a bit more than desirable. I, therefore, went out of the way to bring this point to the notice of Raman's mother and the Chadhas. They said if the girl's family had no objection, why should I raise this question?

Our Wedding Day

My Wife Raman's Parents

Raman and I met and went out on a scooter ride together. We spoke about various things, but I found that she had not given any serious thought to marriage. She thought she was too young for marriage and wished to study further. So, I was not sure if the proposal would be accepted. But her parents persuaded her, telling her that she was only getting engaged at that time and the marriage would take place later. I asked my parents if they approved of the match and even told them (just to make them feel good) that I would not go ahead if they did not approve. On the other hand, my parents kept saying that the family was good and that it had to be my own decision. I took their blessings, and we had a simple engagement ceremony, after which I returned to Bombay.

It was agreed that the marriage would be solemnized after about a year or so, after Raman finished her degree exam in 1965. I returned to Bombay to my job and wrote letters to Raman once in a while. I do not remember if she replied to any of my missives. I visited her once in college. The place had tight security, and they wouldn't let the girls go out, so I had persuaded her mother to accompany me to ensure that I got to meet her.

When I look back and compare the situation of yesteryears to the present times, I feel happy that youngsters today have the freedom to meet and socialize so freely.

Just when we were in the process of finalizing a date for the marriage, the war with Pakistan started. Punjab was the primary sector of fighting. Our plans had, therefore, to be postponed, and once the war was over, we fixed a date in January 1966 - the 9th of January to be precise.

At this point, it would be appropriate to say something about Raman's family and my own. Both my parents were literate but not educated beyond middle school. One reason I accepted the proposal to marry Raman was because her parents were well educated, and my mother-in-law had always been a working woman. My father-in-law, Mohinder Singh Rana, belonged to a well-known family in west Punjab, and his brothers hobnobbed with the British rulers. My father-in-law was the youngest son of the family. He was thoroughly pampered by his four older brothers and two sisters. He was a bit spoilt as a young boy and did not work towards a career.

After they lost everything in the partition of the country and moved to the Indian side of Punjab, he found himself without family wealth and virtually no career. He joined Life Insurance Corporation of India as a field officer and, thereafter through his political connections, became a Revenue officer of the Punjab Government (Hon. Sub Registrar of properties). He was pretty successful in this prestigious position. However, he could not continue in this post for long since he was too honest and upright for the position, which his political bosses used as a source of corrupt money.

His was an eminent family. His cousin, Sardar Ujjal Singh, was an eminent politician who later became the Governor of Punjab and did a stint as Governor of Tamil Nadu. Some other prominent members of my father-in-law's extended family who made a name for themselves include Late Air Chief Marshall Arjan Singh and Khushwant Singh the famous diplomat and writer.

On my mother-in-law's side of the family, Brig. Joginder Singh, and his brother Gurmit (a well-known photojournalist in Bombay who died in a road accident) are some prominent names. My mother-in-law had two sisters. One was Surjit Masi Ji, who married Lt. Col. Charanjit Singh of the Indian Army. They have two children, Satjit Singh, who lives in England, and a daughter Cheeku who lives in the U.S. The other sister, Amar Masi, was married to a senior officer of the Government of India, Ministry of Agriculture. He (Gyan Uncle) was a very nice person whose company I enjoyed immensely. They tragically lost a young son before he was 20, and were left with a daughter, Winnie, our good friend. Winnie is a Ph.D. in nutrition science and teaches in a well-known government institution. She is married to Devinder, a doctor, and has twin daughters, of whom one married Sanj, a delightful young man who lives in England. The other daughter, who became a medical doctor, married a person from Lucknow and is well settled there. I have never met her husband, but I believe he is a sincere man and successful in what he does for a living.

My mother-in-law's brother Mahavir Singh (Mamaji) was a good man who ran a business in Karnal, a city in Haryana. He was very fond of Raman and me. Unfortunately, he died young, and so did one of his sons. The family continues to do well in Karnal. His daughter Preeti married an Army man (Mehra) who retired as a Brigadier and lived in Gurgaon. Mahvair Mamaji's two remaining sons run the business which Mamaji had set up and continue to do well at it. Kanwar, the older son, did a stint in the merchant navy before joining the family business.

Compared to this, my family had a much simpler and more humble background. My father came from a rural family in a village called Maran near Mardan, and my mother came from a trader's family. They were pretty prosperous back in Pakistan, but no one from the family made a mark. They were good middle-class families.

My mother's three brothers were educated and had lucrative businesses before they moved to Delhi after the partition of the Indian subcontinent. She also had two sisters. As I write this, all of them have passed away. The eldest, Sardar Karam Singh, was the head of the family and helped raise the other two brothers to a point. However, as soon as his sons grew up, they started competing with their uncles' sons.

I was very fond of all three of my Mamajis but had a unique personal equation with the eldest —Karam Singh Mamaji. We corresponded regularly till his last days. He was, in a way, the patriarch of the family, and everyone looked up to him for advice. He left behind three sons — Amarjit, Raghbir, Avninder (Nanni) and three daughters. His eldest was a daughter, Swaran Behenji, was sent to Lahore to study medicine. This was a very unusual step in those days (the 1940s), and I thought Mamaji was very modern and progressive to have done this. Swaran Behnji's studies were interrupted by the Partition of India. She finally passed her MBBS from Government Medical College, Amritsar and not from Lahore, which had become a part of Pakistan. She was the first doctor in the family. We kept in touch with her until she died a few years ago. Unfortunately, Mamaji's elder son and all three daughters are no more. The second son (Raghbir, three years older than me) and Nanni are still around and live in Delhi.

As his family expanded, Karam Singh Mamaji insisted the brothers (Mohinder Singh and Joginder Singh) set up on their own. They started their businesses. For a while, they were doing well. However, they fell out, and Joginder Singh, the most educated of the three brothers, walked out and took up a corporate position with Bush Boake Allen, a British manufacturer of flavors and fragrances. He was the company's area manager for north India and did quite well. He later left the company and branched out on his own in the same line of business that his son still runs.

Mohinder Singh Mamaji built a good business and trained his two sons to run it. The sons are doing well and have become grandfathers. I was very close to Mohinder Singh Mama, who treated me like a friend. He often came and stayed with us in Bombay; likewise, I often stayed at their home in Delhi. Unfortunately, I don't share the same warmth with his sons and daughter, and even though we meet at family gatherings, and they show me a lot of respect, we do not share the relationship I had with their father.

The youngest Mama Ji, Joginder Singh and I had good relations and shared an interest in a similar business. I was very fond of him and would always call him wherever I was to enquire about his health and wellbeing. Unfortunately, he also died a couple of years ago. He was the last of the relatives from my mother's side. I miss all my Mamajis but most so Joginder Mama. He had been a good friend, and we shared many professional interests.

Thanks to my marriage to Raman, I would visit Khanna occasionally. Khanna is a medium-sized town located on the G.T. Road between Ambala and Ludhiana. The area and nearby town of Gobindgarh were known for several steel re-rolling mills and various wool knitting factories.

The town had its elite — Sardar Mohinder Singh Khanna, the Bakshis, Dr. Shamsher Singh the famous eye surgeon, Raman's parents—the Ranas, and a few other families. There was a local social club and a cinema, but most social life took place in the homes. Raman's parents, especially her mother Kulwant Rana, were very eminent members of Khanna society and would be invited to any important social event.

Sardar Mohinder Singh Khanna was related to the Ranas - Mrs. Mohinder Singh was my mother-in-law's aunt (Bhuaji), and Bhuaji considered Raman's parents—the Ranas, and a few other families. By virtue of this, I was always invited to their home for at least one meal during my visits.

Since my mother-in-law was educated and had worked with Harvard University's Population Study Group on a project in Punjab, she had interacted with several American doctors and other functionaries who visited to check on the study the group was carrying out in villages near Khanna. Dr. Wyon an

American on the team, his wife, and his children had to live in Khanna during this time. They learned how to speak Punjabi and, through my mother-in-law, came to know all the prominent people of this small town.

Besides a cinema and parties at various people's homes, there was no other social life. Often some residents would travel to Chandigarh or Ludhiana for special shopping or to watch the latest release in cinemas. Since there was no dealer for supplying refills of gas cylinders, my mother-in-law was always on the lookout for someone traveling to Chandigarh to bring a refill. Likewise, when I was visiting, she would get frozen meats — especially chicken, from Chandigarh. Things have changed now, and Khanna has become a bigger commercial hub. Sadly, it is no longer a part of our lives since all the people we knew are either dead or left Khanna.

I must devote a little time here to my mother-in-law. My mother-in-law, Kulwant Rana, was a unique person. She was way ahead of her time, and even though she lived in a small town named Khanna, she had a vision of the world and would fit into any high society group. She had good social graces and was always well groomed.

She worked with the Harvard Population Study Group which ran a project in Punjab and travelled to small villages to collect and collate data about family planning. She was an optimist and believed that any task could be completed if you had the determination. She was open to new ideas and was ambitious. She was always willing to help anyone in need and earned everyone's respect and affection.

Mummy was a great cook, a baker par excellence, and enjoyed entertaining at home. She always had a well-laid table for a meal with the proper cutlery, crisp and laundered napkins, and tablecloth. Mummy and Papa moved to Bangalore later

TRILOK S. GULHATI

and stayed with us. We had the good fortune to serve them and are still receiving their blessings. They both died in our home.

In all my years, having socialized with different kinds of people, I have rarely encountered anyone from a small-town with as much grace and style as my mother-in-law. She was very giving and generous by nature and was very proud of her three children, two boys and a daughter — who became my wife.

I miss you, mom.

My Wife and Her Brothers

9TH JAN, 1966
A SPECIAL DAY

I got married on the 9th of January 1966. We'd had a simple wedding. The wedding party travelled from Chandigarh, where my parents lived. We had hired a bus to take the wedding party to Khanna, where Raman's family lived. We started from Chandigarh with about thirty close relatives, and another eight to ten people joined directly in Khanna.

It was a daytime wedding. We arrived in Khanna at about 1030 am. The wedding party was received with the band-baaja and the Milni took place. An excellent breakfast was laid out for us in a specially erected Shamiana, and then we all moved to the specially set-up pandal that was very beautifully decorated.

The Sikh marriage ceremony (Anand Kraj) is quite a dignified affair. After the ceremony, a sumptuous lunch was laid out, and around 5 pm, we departed for Chandigarh after my bride bid farewell to her parents and friends. She and I travelled in a Chevrolet car, which belonged to my friend Daulat Rai, while the rest of the baraat returned by bus, on which we had travelled in the morning.

When I look at some of the Punjabi weddings of today, I am surprised when I think back to the simplicity of our marriage. I am grateful to my wife's family for making the ceremony simple, dignified, and enjoyable. Likewise, partly due to the non-availability of money, my parents did not have any reception, etc., nor did they have the sangeet and cocktails a day or two before the wedding day, which are now so routine.

We returned to Chandigarh, where my parents lived in a two-bedroom house. They gave us the better of the two rooms, and after a couple of days, we went to Shimla for our honeymoon. Shimla is a hill station town at the height of 6500ft, and usually, one goes there in the summer to avoid the scorching hot weather of the plains. But we could not think of any place better than Shimla since it was not too far.

We stayed at the famous Clarke's Hotel and travelled to Kufri to see and experience snow. We have delightful memories of our brief honeymoon there and of the surroundings such as Kufri (at that time known for winter sports like skiing). Before my marriage, I would often run up to Shimla to escape the heat of the plains. It may sound strange, but I have not revisited Shimla in all these years after our honeymoon. I understand that it is now very urbanized with many apartment buildings and is not as pristine and romantic as it was then.

After our marriage, we travelled to Bombay, where I had to report to work. We had a decent one-bedroom flat on Gamadia Road, which is a road between Peddar Road and Warden Road. There was basic furniture, and I had put in a refrigerator and a cooking facility in the kitchen before I married. When Raman came to Bombay, she was excited to be in a big city and enjoyed the change. She gradually settled into the new life and was very popular with my friends. She was an excellent learner, and I was happy to see her becoming confident and independent in a short while. She managed the house well and was a wonderful hostess to visitors. Her cooking was initially not so great, but she was a fast learner, and in a short time, she became known for her superb sense of taste.

We frequently went to Juhu beach, but my favorite place on a Sunday morning was the Taj coffee shop called the Sea Lounge, where we would end up eating snacks and lingering for 3-4 hours. Quite often, some of our friends would join us there.

After the initial excitement, Raman was bored of sitting at home while I went to work. She was keen to do something but did not know what. For starters, she started exploring the city by bus and would go to the city center — Flora Fountain, Colaba. She was keen to learn to drive, so she joined a driving school. Though she was eager to work and took up different jobs, she did not quite like the jobs or the environment and therefore, did not settle down in any of them.

On my job front, I was in Siemens and was kind of settled, but my heart was not in Engineering Products. My first love was for FMCG products marketing — since I learned selling in Unilever (Hindustan Lever in those days). Also, I was pretty ambitious and told my German boss that I was not too happy with our small flat. Luckily for us, a German expatriate who occupied a house in Bandra went back to Germany, and I managed to have this house allotted to us. This was not a big house but had a large compound — the accommodation size was not much bigger, but it had two bedrooms.

In a city like Bombay, to live in a house with a garden was a luxury only a few lucky ones had. Many people within the company and outside were very envious and would often talk about our parties.

LIFE IN BOMBAY

Besides friends at work (I was in Siemens then), I had some excellent friends like Navin Patel and his wife Lulu Patel, Alyque and Pearl Padamsee, Krishan and Manju Gupta, and many others through these people.

From my workplace, there were some good friends like Mahesh and Siegrid Agarwal, Ranbir, Baljit Sachdeva, and Suresh and Rani Jain. Most of these friendships have continued to thrive over the years. Unfortunately, many of these dear ones are gone as I write this. We are in touch with some of the children of these good people, and even if we do not meet very often, the connections have sustained.

Navin Patel   **Lulu Patel**

Navin and Lulu became very dear and close friends. Navin was a very unusual Gujarati. His father had worked in the railways in the old days. He had died by the time I came to know Navin. Navin was a broad-minded, well-travelled person and had been, at one time, a devoted nationalist who had participated in the freedom struggle. He had hitchhiked from India to London via Afghanistan, Iran, Syria, Greece, and Eastern Europe. He had also done a stint of training with Skoda motors, which was initially a Yugoslavian company. His political heroes were Marshal Tito and Col. Nasser of Egypt, and he had met leaders like Krishna Menon. At the same time, he was active in the India league in London before the independence of India. Naveen was a socialist to the core and supported Ho Chi Minh's struggles when he was fighting the American occupation of south Vietnam.

Parties at Navin's flat in south Bombay and his house in Chembur always had a sprinkling of people from the arts, films, and political arenas. I met some eminent people at his parties: Ram Jethmalani, Khushwant Singh, Charles Correa, and the Israeli consul-general of the time. (India did not recognize Israel for many years, but Israel always had a diplomatic office in Bombay.) I also got to befriend Alyque and Pearl Padamsee (Pearl was the first cousin of Lulu, Navin's wife). Maya and Kali Lal also became our good friends. Kali Lal was at that time the commercial manager with the Swiss Pharma company Sandoz and later moved to Australia with his wife Maya, an Australian citizen.

One of Kali and Maya's favorite pastimes was going to Gaylord's restaurant at Churchgate. In those days, it was a very "elitist" and high-end restaurant. They had a live band, and Kali and Maya were very fond of dancing. Not many Indian couples could dance the Tango in those days. Both Kali and Maya were accomplished dancers, but for me, Tango and many other dances like waltz, Cha Cha Cha, and Foxtrot were new. Maya was a big collector of music from different countries, and for the first time in my life, I was introduced to western classical music and folk music from other parts of the world like Greece, Africa, etc.

After Maya and Kali relocated to Australia, I was in touch with them for some time, but the contact faded. At the time of writing, I am unsure if Kali and Maya are still alive. Even though I have travelled to 89 countries, Australia and New Zealand have eluded me so far. I hope to visit Australia, New Zealand, and a few other places before I die.

Kali was the one who introduced me to Gulab Ramchandani and his wife, Ratna. Gulab was a director of Blue Star, and his wife's family were part-owners of the company. Gulab and Kali had studied at the Doon School together and were friends from their school days. Before my marriage, I would go along with them on weekend excursions. They were fond of camping, and that was my first experience of spending a night in the wilderness in a small tent—a great new experience for me.

I also met many other interesting people, Indians, and foreigners, through Kali and Gulab. All those social interactions were educative since I came from a small town and a low-income family, and the level of sophistication of all these people was awe-inspiring and a learning experience for me.

Gulab later took over as the Headmaster of the Doon School, giving up his business career to help out his Alma Mater which needed a Headmaster, as their search had not yielded any suitable candidate. Gulab and Kali inspired me to send my son Nitesh to Doon School, and I am glad I listened to them, although my wife always regrets having sent him to boarding school (mainly for emotional reasons). Gulab and his wife Ratna contributed a great deal to the modernization of the Doon School and ensured it retained its premium position as the nation's best boarding school. However, it continues to have the elitist badge. As I write this page, both Gulab and his dear wife Ratna (who was an interior designer of repute) are no more. I know that one of their sons followed in his father's footsteps and became a teacher, but I was not up to date on them.

All these experiences added to my growth and the expansion of my horizons. I will always be grateful for their contribution to what I ultimately achieved in life.

"If you tune it so that you have zero chance of failure, you usually also have zero chance of success. The key is to look at ways for when you get to your failure checkpoint, you know to stop."

−Reid Hoffman
Cofounder of LinkedIn

FRIENDS FOREVER

Our lives have been enriched by friendships. Some go back to my youth, some to my professional life, some friends I met serendipitously through life. But without these relationships, I would not be who I became. I owe them all gratitude and would like to remember some of them through these pages.

Mr. Gandhi

One of my earliest friends, apart from friends from school and college, was Mr. Gandhi. His name was Bhagwan Dass Gandhi, but we always called him Gandhi or Gandhi saheb. Gandhi worked in the Sports Department of the Government of Punjab, and I first met him in 1962.

I was in my first job as a stenographer with the Sports Department, located in the basement of the famous Yadavindra Stadium in Patiala. This was the year when I also met several sports celebrities — Balbir Singh, who won the Olympic Hockey Gold medal for India, S. Harbail Singh, who was the coach of the Indian hockey team for the Rome Olympics, and Milkha Singh, when he was preparing for his first outing to Melbourne for the Olympics, as well as many lesser-known athletes from different parts of India.

When I first met Gandhi, I was immediately struck by his wholesome sincerity, dedication to what he was doing, and a big heart. He had a very giving and self-sacrificing nature. We became lifelong friends and kept in touch till he passed away recently. Gandhi was a rare example of what human beings can be. He never said 'no' to anything you asked for and would fulfil your wish even at great inconvenience and sometimes at a high cost to himself. I am in touch with his son, who lives in Ludhiana and has a good business. I was happy to spend a few weeks with him before he died. Rest in peace, my dear Bhagwan Dass

Daulat Rai Chadha

When I first moved to Chandigarh and joined Hindustan Lever as a stenographer, I had to buy a bicycle. So, I went to Bharat Stores in Sector 22. The store belonged to the Chadha family, and two brothers — Daulat Rai and his younger brother Pal ran the store. Daulat Rai and I hit it off immediately, and our friendship blossomed. He was ten years older than me, but we had a tremendous equation.

I soon learned about his family — his parents, wife, and two small children. His father was a retired civil servant, a very upright and conservative man, a stickler for discipline, and kept his two married sons on a very tight rope. No one dared disagree with anything he said or did. He was charming and civil with most outsiders and me and commanded everyone's respect.

Daulat and I shared a common love for reading and keeping updated on international affairs. He was like an elder brother to me; his wife was a wonderful lady and treated me as a family youngster.

Daulat Rai and his wife (Satya Bhabhi) became excellent friends of mine and later played an important role in my life. I also got along well with the other members of the family and have kept in touch with all of them. My friend Daulat Rai died a few years ago. He is survived by his son Ruby and his family. I also keep in touch with Jack, the youngest Chadha brother, who lives in Bombay.

The Suris

Gurdial Singh Suri was the eldest of four brothers. He was a manager in a bank in Chandigarh. I made his acquaintance via Daulat Rai Chadha, and we became such good friends that even though he has passed away, I continue to cherish a deep friendship with his son Baba Suri and his grandson Jaideep.

Suri Sahib was a sincere, reasonable, and dependable friend. Soon I came to know his entire family, and during our visit to England, I also met his brother Gurdev who was, at that time, a retired (but spirited) British government employee. One extraordinary thing about Suri sahib which I remember, is that he never ate any fruits. On the other hand, in my family, we are great fruit-eaters. Whenever someone came home, my mother would

bring out the fruit platter to offer them — always forgetting that Mr. Suri did not eat any fruit. He was the only person I knew who had such a dislike for fruits. We recently met his wife, who is still alive and in reasonably good health and now lives with her daughter in the U.S. Baba lives in Delhi, but his son Jaideep and his wife live in Bangalore.

Daulat Rai Chadha, Suri sahib and I were a trio — we were often together and would go out and have a beer once in a while at the Mount View Hotel in Chandigarh.

Unfortunately, these old friends are no longer there, but I often miss them and think of our great times together.

The Sethis and Salujas

Kailash Chand Saluja   **Mr. Sethi**

We met the Salujas when we moved into our flat in Heritage Estate. Our flat was in the 14th block and both Sethi and Saluja families lived in the same block.

Kailash Chand Saluja or Saluja Saheb as we called him, and his wife Premji became good friends.

Saluja saheb had retired as General Manager of Bombay telephones, during which period he had also done a stint in Botswana (southern Africa) helping that country's telephone establishment.

We (Sethis, Salujas and us) became close and often played cards together, sometimes joined by others.

The Salujas have two children — their daughter Jyoti who is married to a wonderful person Rakesh Kapila lives in Belgium and runs a lucrative business. During my travels in Europe, I have spent some enjoyable time with the family in their lovely home outside Brussels. Saluja Saheb's son is an excellent marketing person and is currently General Manager of Times of India at Bangalore and is doing well. He lives with his parents — a win-win for all of them.

Saluja Saheb is a few years older than me and has been in generally good health but for a troubling knee.

Salujas, like us and our common friend (late) Sethi saheb, moved out of Heritage, and have excellent homes next to each other in a very good part of Bangalore, fortunately not too far from us.

Bagu Ochaney

I met Bagu while he was working at Lintas in Bombay. We took an instant liking to one another and became good friends. Bagu was on the client-service side of Lintas and was very successful. Whenever I visited Bombay, I would meet him.

Bagu is a Sindhi Sikh who wears a turban and has a flowing white beard, making him look like a very impressive Sikh preacher. When I first met him, he had a more urban look, his beard neatly tied up, and he wore a necktie to work.

While he has been a devout Sikh and has always kept the Guru Granth Sahib in his home, he enjoys his two drinks of whisky every evening and has a modern outlook. Bagu is a highly principled person — sometimes even annoyingly so. He married the wonderful Manjula and the couple have been good friends with my wife Raman and me. Bagu and Manjula moved to Canada for a few years where I visited and stayed with them for a few days but have recently moved back to Bangalore.

Bagu's wife, Manjula held an important position in Walmart and was head of procurement of home fashions like linen, bedroom wear, and artefacts for bedrooms. Since Manjula's family is from Bangalore, they decided to retire here, and they have a beautiful home that we visit every once in a while.

Sunil and Shiela Thakurdas

I first met Sunil Thakurdas when my head office asked me to interview him for a job in Gabriel, India, where I was the Regional Manager in Delhi. Sunil had just finished college and was looking for a job and must have sent his CV to my company in Bombay.

I spoke to him for about 30 minutes, found him quite suitable for the job, and recommended that he be taken.

Sunil was a product of the famous St. Stephen's College in Delhi. He was a smart young man with a good disposition. Both of Sunil's parents were educationists. His father Frank Thakurdas was well known in Delhi's academic circles. Both he and Sunil's mother were professors at the well-known Kirorimal College.

When we moved to Bombay a few years later, Sunil became a good friend. He then changed jobs and joined Richardson Hindustan (part of Richard Merril). Sunil soon announced his wedding to the beautiful Sheila who was his colleague. We attended their wedding reception at the Radio Club in Mumbai.

Sunil Thakurdas

Many years later Sunil joined SKF and was posted in Bangalore. We had also moved to Bangalore and so got to meet more often. The friendship grew to a special one over the years. Sunil and Shiela have two children — son Nikhil and daughter Nishita — both of whom are successful and happily married with children. Nikhil runs a travel agency in Pune and Nishita has her brand of fashion products, ceramics, etc.

Sunil was a regular at the Bangalore Club and could be seen there almost every day. He would spend time there with his friends over a couple of beers. Sadly, Sunil passed away a few years ago. His wife divides her time between Bangalore where her daughter lives, and Pune where her son and family are settled. Sunil and I shared a strong bond for over 50 years. I miss him and think of him often.

"An investment in knowledge pays the best interest."

-Benjamin Franklin
Statesman, Diplomat, Writer

MARDAN HOUSE

When we lived in Bombay, I could not even imagine owning an apartment. The prices for even a modest-sized apartment were beyond our capacity. Having lived in Central and South Bombay all along, we could not imagine living in the suburbs.

Before we could even think of investing in an apartment, we moved to Bangalore, and Bangalore in 1972 did not have very many apartments. Most people lived in independent houses. We were given accommodation by the company. It was a beautiful 3-bedroom house with a lovely garden and car park - a refreshing change from the apartment in Bombay. The children enjoyed the spacious house, and the neighborhood. It was a wonderful area with beautiful bungalows, open spaces, and a lake nearby.

I was always restless and wanted more out of my career. I felt stifled in a job and wanted to do something on my own. I decided to quit, as a result of which we were homeless overnight. We were asked to move out of the house given by the company by a specific date. We searched for an affordable place in the same neighborhood but weren't lucky. I was in a fix since we could not find the right kind of accommodation by that deadline. I was too proud to seek an extension although my wife and some friends suggested that.

Luckily our friends, Dr., and Mrs. Sengupta, said they were going to England for 4-6 months and offered us their flat in another neighborhood not far from where we lived. It was a small first floor flat, and the landlord's family lived on the ground floor. We felt very grateful and relieved and gladly accepted Debi Sengupta's offer. We packed all our stuff, put it in the company-house's garage, and moved to our friends' furnished flat. While this was an excellent stop-gap arrangement, we had to find a place we could call our own.

With a temporary roof over our heads, we had the luxury of some time to look for a home to live in.

Luckily before the Senguptas returned, we found a place on the first floor of a bungalow in Sadashivnagar. It was an excellent two-bedroom apartment with an open terrace, perfect for our needs. The owners, an older man, and his wife, lived on the ground floor. We lived in this apartment for some time but had endless troubles with the landlord, who even objected to me having a shower late at night when I returned from work. It was time to begin house hunting again.

In the meantime, I had set up a factory to manufacture spice extracts in partnership with two friends.

We went to Bangalore Club frequently and would spend Sunday mornings sitting by the poolside. While the children swam, I enjoyed a beer or two. We became friends with a family who had recently moved from East Africa. They ran a soft drink business and had good connections with the liquor industry. When I mentioned that I was looking for a house to rent, preferably in the same area where we lived, the gentleman surprised me by pulling out a key from his pocket. The key belonged to a house in the same area where we lived (Sadashivnagar/RMV Extension) and was owned by a friend of the gentleman who lived in Chennai. The owner of the house, Mr. Palani, lived in Chennai and was looking for a tenant for his home.

So, within a few days after the chat in Bangalore Club, we moved to 21 Rajmahal Vilas Extension. This was an unfinished house — the ground floor, which was complete, consisted of three bedrooms, a dining area, a living room, and a kitchen as well as a beautiful little garden near the car park. The house was more than enough for our family and a significant improvement from the apartment we lived in before this. My mother also moved in with us after my father's death and this house was more than comfortable for all of us to live in.

We lived at this address for almost 12 years. The house saw the birth of our third child Sonira, our eldest Soyna going off to college, and our son Nitesh leaving for boarding school. After 12 years of wonderful memories, we received a notice from the landlord to vacate. We were once again on a house-hunting spree. Finally, I found a very nice big, brand-new house in RMV II Stage, where we moved. At this point I realized that it was important for us to have a home of our own.

My mother was also keen that I have a home of my own for our family. We then looked for a plot of land and found a small house built on a good size (50ft x 80ft) plot. It was a very simple house and not built to our specifications. The place was conveniently located with several shops and a large hospital close by. (M. S. Ramaiah Medical College Hospital).

We realized that we would need to redesign the house and sought an expert opinion from an architect. The architect we engaged recommended demolishing the existing house and building a new modern one. While my business was now doing well, we still did not have enough money to build a house.

We began building the house with some money we had saved and parallelly applied to LIC Housing for a loan. The construction was slow, but we finally had our own home. We moved there in November of 1994 with some parts of the house still unfinished. We had a debate in the family about naming the house. There were several suggestions, but finally, we chose the name Mardan House — named after the city in Pakistan where I was born. The name stuck and even today references to "Mardan House" come up.

Mardan house had four large bedrooms, a large living area and family dining room, a modern kitchen, and a pooja room.

The house was designed in such a way that the living and dining areas were both connected to the garden. This was an advantage particularly when we entertained. We made a lot of memories with friends and family there.

The neighborhood was upmarket, and some eminent people lived on our street. Our neighbors were Mr. Patil, Chief Secretary, and Mrs. Margret Alva, a central minister. The Kulkarni family who lived on the same street as us became good friends.

Several significant events in our life happened while we lived in Mardan House. My mother-in-law who lived with us since the early 90's passed away here. Our son Nitesh and daughter Sonira both got married there. Sonira's son Agastya spent the first couple of months of his life with us here.

"Start as small as you can. When I started SkinnyMe Tea, I had $24 in the bank, and I was entirely self-funded. If you are not embarrassed by the first version of your product; you've launched too late."

—Gretta Rose van Riel
Founder of Hey Influencers

THE ENTREPRENEUR'S
JOURNEY STARTS

(Mr. Trilok Gulhati passed away before he could write this chapter. It was put together by Meena Raghunathan, through conversations with Mrs. Raman Gulhati, Mr. Nitesh Gulhati, Dr. Soyna Gulhati, and Ms. Sonira Monish. To that extent, it does suffer with gaps, but hopefully not too many mistakes. The chapter gives an overview of the start of the entrepreneurial journey and tries to provide a context to the narrative in the next chapter.)

Trilok had been working for some years with Reckitt Colman, when suddenly, the company transferred him to (then) Calcutta. He definitely did not want to shift himself and his family around at this stage. Anyway, for some time now, he had been considering taking the entrepreneurial plunge. The transfer-discussion tipped the situation, and he decided to resign and start out on his own.

But what enterprise could he start? Those were the license-permit raj days. There were few things that an entrepreneur could do. It was at this stage that Mr. M.S. Srinivasan, an old friend, and senior bureaucrat, came to his rescue. Through him, Trilok got a list of possible industries he could start up. And from this list, he narrowed down on the manufacture of oleoresin.

Oleoresins are semi solid extracts composed of resin and essential or fatty oils. These extracts come from spices such as basil, capsicum, ginger, pepper, etc. Organic solvents like ethanol, ethyl acetate or ethylene dichloride are used to extract the oleoresins from the spices. It is a complex manufacturing process. Most oleoresins are used widely as flavors and perfumes, including in the manufacture of food products.

Trilok decided to go in for the manufacture of oleoresin from black pepper for use in the processed food industry. He founded a company called Sonit. It was a small operation to begin with, and an extraction unit was put in Peenya Industrial Estate.

The small team worked night and day. The problems were myriad. Bank financing was always a challenge. And then the manufacturing process itself—the unit could not achieve the quality required for the market, and the market was dominated by American competitors whose quality was very high. Moreover, the margins were very thin.

Survival was a challenge. There were no luxuries or indulgences for the family—the kids did without the things that their friends took for granted. There were days when there was not enough money even to fill the car's petrol tank. There were big loans hanging on Trilok's head and servicing them every month was not easy.

But sheer persistence kept him going. All the time, he was reaching out to people and discussing possibilities. It was at this time that one of the customers of Sonit, a Greek company called Vioryl SA, counselled the family that oleoresins was a very difficult business, and they would find it very difficult to meet the necessary quality standards. Their contact suggested that they shift to making flavors and fragrances, and even offered to help with technology and training.

This seemed like a great opportunity. Trilok and Raman went to Greece to see the plant, process etc., and Raman stayed back to learn the technology. With her background in Chemistry and her intuitive understanding of flavors, it was a home-coming for her. On her return to India, she along with one chemist, started up a company called Sonarome for the manufacture of flavors and fragrances. Sonarome operated out of a small house in Rajmahal Vilas, Bangalore.

They started out by making Vioryl flavors and fragrances. But those were for the European market, and too subtle for the Indian taste. Raman started researching and innovating. Based on her intensive studies, she started coming out with new flavors and scents. These gained traction with customers.

However, marketing was a huge challenge. Raman was a gifted flavorist, and her products were excellent. But she had neither the interest nor the time to market them. The company just about survived and had sales of about Rs.1 lakh. But then it hit a wall. It was obvious that things could not go on like this.

This is when the obvious struck Raman. There was an ace-marketer right at home! She persuaded Trilok to close down Sonit and join Sonarome. He did, and the sales went up five times that year!

Now, Sonarome started to establish itself both in terms of its innovative and quality products, as well as marketing. The company started with culinary essences for home-use—basically 25 ml packs. They had flavors such as vanilla, strawberry, chocolate, etc.

The first big successful flavor was pineapple which was developed in 1983 and is still a best-seller! Then came flavors for chewing gums.

With all these popular products, the company sales started picking up, but along the way came the realization that their costs were very high due to the packaging—the real profits would come only if they moved to bulk packing. And so, they made the move, and from being a Business-to-Consumer company, moved to a Business-to-Trade operation, before moving to Business-to-Business. This was when things really started picking up. Trilok's untiring efforts saw the markets expanding to Mumbai, Delhi, Calcutta, and Gujarat.

Another challenge of that period (1980s and '90s) was the question of raw materials. A significant portion of Sonarome's raw materials were imported. In 1990 came the foreign exchange crisis and the company suffered seriously as a consequence. At this time Trilok got the idea of exporting so that they could earn foreign exchange. With his marketing prowess, he could find buyers for his flavors in Malaysia, Sri Lanka, and other Asian countries. Then came a breakthrough in East Africa—this opened up a huge market. The foreign exchange generated through the sales was used to buy raw material.

But it was not all smooth sailing. Bank loans - whether for expansion, for buying land and creating infrastructure, for operations - were almost impossible to come by, and this was a constant source of stress and worry for Trilok and took up most of his time.

Another big jolt came in the shape of trusted people letting the company down. The most emotionally difficult incident, which also set the company back seriously, was the experience with an employee called Manjunath.

He had been hired as a Purchase Manager in 1999. He soon gained everyone's trust and was given responsibilities such as going to the Bank for routine matters like depositing cheques, cash, and DDs on behalf of the Company, etc. He used to collect the day's cash, cheques, demand drafts from the Accounts team, and go to the bank to deposit the same.

He would also sit at other people's computers during lunch. A new employee, Rajani, found this a bit odd. She started digging into things and found a manipulated bank counterfoil.

Rajani alerted Raman, and they started systematically investigating the matter, and found several fake counterfoils. What Manjunathan had been doing was depositing say Rs. 400 in the bank but manipulating the counterfoil to read Rs. 56,400! He has been discounting the cheques and drafts through a local broker. As the investigation went on, it was discovered that several sales proceeds were not deposited into the Company account at all. It was obvious that Manjunath had fellow conspirators, and the accountant was also found to be part of the fraud. The auditors too had obviously been part of the cover-up.

It also came to light that Manjunath had floated a company and was buying raw materials needed by Sonarome, and then selling them to Sonarame at highly inflated prices.

`The accountant was suspended, the auditor was changed, and an FIR filed against Manjunath, as a result of which he went to jail. While it was a valuable lesson on not to trust anyone blindly, the money itself was never recovered.

It was at this stage that Trilok's son Nitesh took the decision to leave his job in the US in order to help manage the company. He first moved to Dubai as part of Sonarome, and then to India in 2008, and has been hands-on in the company since then.

The Manjunath episode led to review and formalization of systems and processes and tightening all aspects of administration and finance. It also led to Nitesh getting involved full-time in the operations, which brought in new ways of doing things. The episode, sad as it was, could thus be said to have laid the foundation for the growth of Sonarome as a professional company.

TALKING BUSINESS

(This part of the narrative refers to the early years of Sonarome.)

My business had started in a small shed measuring 1750 sq. ft., which housed my office, a small lab, and our production facility. Soon after the business started growing, we acquired the next shed, and later built a modern multi-story structure between the two sheds.

This building housed our offices and flavor and fragrance labs. Simultaneously, we also acquired another shed behind the second shed and separated the fragrance production. We now had a manufacturing facility of 4000 sq. ft., an office, and a lab with an additional 4200 sq. ft. We were growing at a rapid pace, and I could see it wouldn't be long before we ran short of space. That happened faster than I had thought. So, we rented another place nearby and used it as a warehouse.

This only confirmed my belief that we needed a large piece of land where we could build a brand-new facility. Therefore, we started looking for industrial land in and around our location. We felt that if we had 2 acres (80000 sq. ft. plot) built wisely, we would be OK for our future growth.

I soon discovered that the land prices in Peenya Industrial Area and other recognized areas were unaffordable. This led us to look at different locations far from town. Some brokers suggested we look at land in the Doddaballapur Industrial Area, which was in an entirely different direction from the city. I saw a piece of land with a small factory on it. This land area was more than three times what we were looking for (250,000 sq. ft.). I liked it but wanted my wife's opinion.

The property was in an upcoming industrial area close to the new airport, which was coming up in the north of Bangalore. It was on the map, well connected to the airport and the national highway. It was an old watch dial factory that had been lying closed for 12 years. The previous owner could not make a success of the business and had removed all machinery.

The broker who showed us the property gave me the name and address of the owner who lived in Kolkata. I decided to travel to Kolkata and meet the owner, Mr. Dalmia. I usually stayed with my friends Indrajit and Mungla on Ritchie Road. Indrajit asked me if I had any specific objective for my trip. When I mentioned to him that the purpose of the visit was to meet a gentleman called Mr. Dalmia, Indrajit said that he knew him very well. Mr. Dalmia's father was a well-known cardiologist and a member of the Saturday Club where my friends socialized often. He told me that they were good people. I was happy to hear this and more confident now that I would have a fair deal.

Audience with Mother Teresa in Kolkata

The next day I met Sanjay Dalmia and expressed my desire to buy his Bangalore industrial land. He was friendly but discouraged me from buying the property and mentioned that there were a lot of complications and pending issues. When I asked him to elaborate, he said the Government of Karnataka had threatened to take back the property since there had been no activity for more than ten years. He said he had filed a writ petition in Karnataka High Court restraining the Government.

He also said he owed the state electricity board some money, had issues with the village panchayat and owed some money to the industrial area's development board.

When I asked him what efforts he had made to solve those problems, he said, "I live in Kolkata, and unless you are close by and have contacts with various departments of the Government, you cannot solve the problems." I explained to him that I was based in Bangalore and that I had connections with some senior government officials, and that I could perhaps help him solve all those problems. I wanted him to agree on a price after which I could begin sorting out all the issues, for which he would have to bear the costs. We decided on a price of Rs. 2.15 crores. I shook hands with him and returned to Bangalore.

I then went to see a senior IAS officer who worked with KIADB and explained the situation to him. He said that it would be best if Mr. Dalmia withdrew the petition he had filed in the high court and paid the dues he owed to the Government. I informed Mr. Dalmia of this conversation, and he then instructed his lawyer to withdraw the petition.

I then asked the Department to issue a demand notice for the arrears standing against the property and offered to pay on Dalmia's behalf. I settled the Electricity Board dues and sorted out pending issues with the village Panchayat. A friend, who was a senior officer with the government and helping me sort out these issues, asked me whether I was sure if Mr. Dalmia would honor the deal. This got me worried and then I requested the officer concerned to issue a letter to Mr. Dalmia stating that the Department was willing to have all issues sorted out on the condition that the property is transferred to our company Sonarome. This was a great favor from the senior officer, and I have always felt grateful to him.

To cut the long story short, all the above was achieved and I now needed money to settle the matter. So, I went to my bank and excitedly explained our plans to acquire this big property which I assured them would help me grow the business into a large organization. But the banker, being a banker, told me that giving me any loan to buy that property was impossible since my balance sheet numbers were still very small. I was devastated and said to the bank manager, "Why do I need a bank if you cannot help me in my situation?." But nothing would change his mind.

I was in a crisis and could not think of any way to raise Rs. 2 crores. It was a stressful situation, and I was at a dead end.

I then remembered that I had met with Mr. Jaspal Bindra, the Asia-Pacific Head of Standard Chartered Bank with which we did business. This had been at a party which my wife and I were invited to in Bombay. The bank had sponsored our trip there since we were one of their early business accounts and an example of a successful family-owned business.

Since I did not have any other source, I called the regional head of Standard Chartered bank in Singapore to seek his help. Unfortunately, he was unavailable, so I spoke to his secretary and asked her to give me his email address — which she graciously did.

In my email, I explained to Mr. Jaspal Bindra that I needed a loan from his bank to grow my business. I explained that I saw this as an opportunity to put my company on a fast growth track, and that I would repay the loan in 6-8 months. My e-mail had the desired impact. The very next day I received a call from the local bank asking me when I needed the money. This was a turning point in the history of Sonarome.

With Nobel Laureate Yunus Khan in Singapore

The rest is history — we bought the property, the business grew at a rapid pace, and we were able to return the bank loan with interest in precisely eight months, much to the surprise of the bank. We were on our way to realizing my dream of becoming a world-class company — no matter how small.

The move to the new location had proved immensely useful. We added a lot more equipment and were able to handle large orders. We added a modern and well-managed warehouse. We set up our own spray drying plant as well as an Effluent Treatment Plant. We also added a brand-new office building to the premises and moved our flavor, fragrance, and Quality Control (QC)/Regulatory labs into spacious modern buildings. We also set up a Microbiology lab as part of our Quality Control (QC)/regulatory needs.

Today, Sonarome flavors are used nationwide, by major companies in buttermilk seasoning, in biscuits, candies, noodle masala, soft drinks, etc. If you have a cooling summer drink or satisfy your sweet tooth with a cookie or candy, there is a good chance that there is a Sonarome flavor in there!

Sonarome, like most other enterprises, went through enormous ups-and-downs. From struggling for survival, to making mistakes and setting them right, Trilok and Raman showed courage, guts, and persistence in meeting every challenge.

Today Sonarome is at the forefront of the flavors and fragrances sector in India. Its natural solutions are sourced from natural derivatives like plants and trees and have nature-identical features. Its vision is '...a world of flavors and fragrances which reaches the perfection that is innate in nature.' Sonarome aims at being able to blend the myriad aromas and flavors that exist and combine it with technology to tap into the recesses of nature. It has a sharp focus on sustainability and works to create transparent and fair supply chains that deliver sustainable and regenerative food ingredients. This provides impactful market opportunities for SMEs, smallholder farmers, indigenous people, women, and youth.

By 2015, Sonarome had grown to a multi-crore company and a leader among Indian flavor companies. Trilok was now looking for a strategic buyer. After a long search, 60 per cent stake of the company was sold to Frutarom/IFF. However, the values and culture of the buyer did not gel with the founder-family. Hence, they bought back the stake, and sold it to the French company Robertet, which was a better fit.

Sonarome is rated among the top Indian Flavors and Fragrances companies, selling its products to over 4,000 businesses in India and 45 countries across the globe. It continues to grow from strength to strength and maintains its pre-eminent position in the flavors and fragrances industry and continues to strive for excellence and market leadership. Raman and Nitesh continue to be closely involved in providing leadership to the company.

MY WIFE, RAMAN

Raman and I first met in Chandigarh. At the time she was still in college pursuing a degree in Chemistry. I found her attractive and intelligent. Although timid, she seemed like someone who was curious and interested in learning new things. She had been a good student and is one of the few people I know who still remembers what she learned in college.

Hailing from a small town, Raman was very new to the world's ways and had no idea how the business world worked. Most men in her extended family had been either in the defence forces or traders. She had no idea how private companies or corporates worked.

Raman

When we returned to Bombay after our marriage, for a while, she was busy setting up a new home but soon showed a tremendous desire to do and learn new things. She wanted to learn to drive a car, learn to paint, wanted to work, and socialize as if moving from a small town in Punjab to Bombay was something she was cut out for.

While I went to the office, she explored Bombay independently, and soon got comfortable travelling by bus, local trains, etc., and interviewed for some odd jobs. This was quite an eye-opener for me since I had seen wives of some friends who did not dare to move out of their homes without their husbands, not to speak of taking a local bus or train alone. That impressed me and I encouraged her to be as independent as possible.

For household work, we initially had a male servant named Chandan (from my bachelor days) who could do odd jobs around the house and cook (or help in cooking). I had taken him to Punjab to attend my wedding.

Soon Chandan started resenting the control my wife wished to exercise over him. He was used to being his boss since, as a bachelor, I would be away the whole day, and he would have the place to himself. Now my wife was his boss and questioned everything he did. She did not have patience with Chandan's sloppiness and poor hygiene, and soon we had to let Chandan Singh leave. We had a part-time "Bai" who would come, clean up and do the laundry.

That transferred the chores of cooking, shopping, etc., to Raman. As I write this, we have been married for over 50 years. Raman has been a perfect wife, an excellent mother to our three children, and Nani/Dadi to the grandchildren. Raman has also been a wonderful and productive partner in the business. She has an excellent sense of taste and smell and has helped our company Sonarome grow with several winning formulations. She continues to play an important role and now has a team of 12 flavorists and application assistants.

Raman is by nature hardworking and is always busy at work and home. She is a loving mother and grandmother, a good friend, cook par excellence, community leader, and a no-nonsense person who can easily handle complex problems. She is compassionate beyond measure. She ensures to take care of the less-privileged - the poor, domestic help, and the lower-level workers in the factory. My son jokingly refers to her as the family's "socialist." She is also in charge of the family's investments (This works well because I have no head for or interest in money and I would rather spend my time building an organization, creating a company image, and worrying about business growth.)

Raman also has a good sense of aesthetics regarding home décor and is quite house-proud. By the grace of the Almighty, we are both in reasonably good health (considering our ages). Raman has learned to live with her asthma and continues to take the support of whatever new treatments medical science has to offer. I have lived through a heart attack, a little episode with the brain, and a few minor age-related problems. Fortunately, I do not have classic diseases like hypertension, high cholesterol, or diabetes. We both do light exercise —

mainly walking and yoga; we follow regulated diets, and ensure we go for regular and timely medical check-ups.

Recently she has taken to golf with tremendous passion, and I do hope she does more and more of it, partly because she enjoys the game but also because it makes her go into the open where she breathes fresh air and has the necessary walk.

Raman and I are blessed with three highly educated, well-settled children with wonderful spouses, and six loving grandchildren. Two of the children — my son and younger daughter living within 5 minutes walking distance from our home. We are also blessed since, even at this age, we are profitably engaged and continue to work. Another blessing is that our place of work is close by, and we do not spend endless hours commuting.

We are indeed grateful to God for all this.

Three Generations of the Gulhati Family

"Passion, creativity, and resilience are the most crucial skills in business. If you've got those, you're ready to embark on the journey."

–Jo Malone
Founder of Jo Malone

KAL-AAJ-KAL

I nurture mixed feelings as I sit down and write the concluding chapters of my book. I turned 84 last year, and being gainfully engaged even at this age is a matter of great satisfaction. I feel blessed to be able to go to work five days a week. Raman and I completed 57 years of marriage this year. Despite all our initial struggles, Raman and I have been blessed with a happy life. With reasonably good health and no financial worries, we hope and pray that in the remaining years we will enjoy the same degree of comfort.

Sonarome - It all started here.
Shed No. C-136 in Peenya

I enjoy my role as Chairman of the Sonarome company, which we jointly founded and nurtured. We celebrated 40 years of Sonarome last year and are grateful that, over time, Sonarome has become a name to reckon with in our line of business. I still work with the same passion that I had in my youth. During the pandemic when most people were working from home, we were going to the factory taking the necessary precautions.

I do not know how long I will continue to work. A few years ago, we sold the majority equity in the company to an Israeli

My current Sonarome Office

company (*Frutarom*), who, in turn, sold to IFF, a US-based company. Through this merger, we became part of IFF — which is a massive monolith of a company.

Unlike Frutarom, which had no presence in India (and we became the face of Frutarom in India), IFF has been in the country for over 50 years and has manufacturing units, offices, and labs in multi-locations in the country. We still own 30 per cent of Sonarome, but IFF has the option to acquire it (of course, at today's valuation). The question is whether they would like us to continue running the company beyond 2022. I am prepared for both situations — if they want me to continue to work for another 2-3 years, I will be glad to do so (subject to good health of course). On the other hand, if they want me to retire and have one of their people at the helm, I am mentally quite prepared for that. (*The family subsequently bought back shares from IFF and then re-sold it to the French company Robertet. Raman and Nitesh continue to be involved full-time.*)

On the personal front, we bow our heads to Waheguru as all three of our children are well educated and well-settled now with their own families. We as parents feel blessed to see them growing as good citizens with a profound sense of compassion for the needy, and dutiful toward their parents. Each of our children has their own perspective and their own set of values and express their love towards us in their own unique way. To our delight, our son and daughter and their families meet us almost every day. Sonira's husband Monish and their children Agastya and Shanaya are a great source of joy to both Raman and me.

Our Three Children, Sonira, Nitesh, and Soyna.

Our house is surrounded by greenery, and we enjoy the company of some good neighbors. Although we don't travel much, we are located very close to the international airport, and my office is only 10 minutes from our home.

At this age, we really feel blessed to have six grandchildren who are growing in front of our eyes and creating their own identities. Nitesh and Jaspreet have a daughter and a son. Aanya, their daughter has just graduated from NYU, and their son, Naylin, has just joined Babson College in Boston.

With Sonira at Disneyworld

My Talented Daughter Sonira Gulhati in 1998

Sonira's Family

Sonira and Monish's son, Agastya, is a gifted child and will soon be out of high school to chart his chosen path. He is an exceptional child with a strong interest in history and tremendous potential. Their youngest daughter, Shanaya, is our youngest grandchild. She is just eight but an amazingly mature child and knows what she wants in life. We are very fond of her, and she too shares a very strong bond with the two of us.

Soyna had a delayed pregnancy. She has two exceptionally smart twin girls- Emma and Olivia. At the age of 11, they seem to be mature young ladies, doing so well at school and knowing what they want in life. Soyna and Courtney live in a beautiful home in Colorado, USA. I have not got a chance to visit them yet but hope to if my health permits. I do wish I could see them more often. It is so satisfying to see that all our children have a comfortable life with no serious financial worries.

My Daughter Dr. Soyna and Son-In-Law Courtney

Soyna's Twin Daughters

My son Nitesh and his wife Jaspreet

Nitesh's daughter Aanya

My wife and I thoroughly believe in the Sikh doctrine of Daswand (as per the Sikh faith, one should donate dasvandh—that, one tenth of one's income, both financially (as a tithe) and directly in the form of seva), and Wand Ke Khao (to share the fruits of one's labor with others before considering oneself) and have always contributed to charity in every possible way.

We hope our children will also practice seva bhav and compassion and do good for others.

Trilok Gulhati passed away on 15th July 2023.

"Embrace what you don't know, especially in the beginning, because what you don't know can become your greatest asset. It ensures that you will absolutely be doing things different from everybody else."

–Sara Blakely
Founder of Spanx, Inc

SONAROME FOUNDATION

(Sonarome Foundation, the services arm of Sonarome, was close to Trilok's heart. However, he had not set down anything about it. Hence, this section, based on interviews by Meena Raghunathan with Ms. Raman Gulhati, has been added to elaborate on something important to him.)

Q. Mr. Trilok Gulhati has mentioned the Sonarome Foundation in his writing. You have been deeply involved in this. Can you tell us more about it?

Well, I suppose it started with my deep desire to do something for society, to give back to those who were less privileged. I could see the travails of the communities around us - the lack of quality education or healthcare, the poverty—and I wanted to do something.

Around this time, my husband and son met an airhostess during a flight. This European lady was devoting every minute of her spare time and large amounts of her money to a community project she had initiated in Bangladesh, having been moved by the poverty she saw there. (This initiative has sustained and grown into an important development program there). When they mentioned our desire to contribute to society, she had only one thing to say, 'Start near you, start small.'

We took this to heart and to this day, the Sonarome Foundation, that was started in 2006, continues to work with our communities around our factory.

But even with this guidance, to start with, I was not sure what the best path to take was. Let me tell you about the beginnings. It may sound strange, but many years ago, a friend, our doctor and I had just loaded a few chairs and a table into the car and went to a nearby village. We set out the chairs under a tree and sat there for a few hours, asking passers-by if they had any health problems, if they wanted to get their BP checked, if they wanted a doctor consultation. That day, about 15 people came to us. We started doing this on a weekly basis.

One day, the principal of the government school nearby asked us what we were doing and who we were. We explained, and the dynamic lady told us that we could use the school premises for our health check-ups, as we were working for the good of the community. That was a big help.

Slowly, more and more people started coming to us. Through our frequent visits to the school, we also began to understand the situation of the school, the quality of education etc. We started contributing small infrastructure, furniture, plates, and utensils for the mid-day meal etc. The principal mentioned to us that the children came to school hungry, and their first meal was the school-lunch served to them. This also impacted their learning. We were saddened by this situation. We decided to do something about it. We started sending them supplies of a nutritious ganji (porridge) mix which they could cook and serve as a hot breakfast every day. We also sent someone to train the school cook in how to cook and serve this, keeping hygiene in mind.

These activities in Veerapura were the first small steps we took.

Q: Since that beginning, you have done a lot. What are some of your key initiatives?

We have expanded our activities to nine villages around our factory. Our doctor covers each village in a weekly schedule and anyone who is ill can get a consultation and medicines. He has access to almost 200 types of generic medicines. We also ensure to supply BP and Sugar medicines to chronic patients.

We are working with the schools in these villages—from giving computers and facilitating e-learning, to infrastructure development, to supporting school-trips for the children. We have helped schools build toilets, classrooms, and stages for events, and provided play equipment. We found that parents wanted their children to learn English and computers. The students themselves were also eager to do this. But there were no teachers. We have appointed teachers for these subjects in most of our partnered schools. Recently, we have appointed a Hindi teacher in one of the schools! These teachers are on the rolls of the Sonarome Foundation and provide quality input in the schools.

We have recently contributed for a swimming pool in a government school, and hope that the children from around the area are able to take advantage of the facility to learn this important skill.

We also contribute to the activities of a few select NGOs, to enable them to spread their good work.

Q: Doing something for the community has always been important for you both. You see Sonarome Foundation as an important part of life and the work of yourself and your husband Mr. Trilok Gulhati. Why is this?

I have always been passionate about doing my bit and giving back to society. Poverty and lack of access disturb me deeply. This is the reason why I have always wanted to do what I could. My mother, in her day, did a lot for society. Back in the times when women, especially in small places in Punjab, did not do much outside the house, she was always in the community, working and volunteering for various causes.

I think that in the case of Trilok, the hardships that he saw when he was young must have been a motivation to try to alleviate suffering.

The concepts of seva and dasvandh (giving a tenth of one's wealth to charity) of our Sikh faith have also been a constant reminder to both of us in regard to our duties to society.

Q. What lies ahead?

Doing more and reaching out to more people every year. Even as Sonarome Foundation continues to grow, I am also in the process of setting up another entity, as sometimes CSR regulations can constrain activities. Through the TS Gulhati Charitable Trust, which is in the making, we can reach more people and take up different kinds of activities.

"The key to realizing a dream is to focus not on success but on significance — and then even the small steps and little victories along your path will take on greater meaning."

–Oprah Winfrey
Global media leader, producer, and actress

MY TAKE ON LIFE

Looking back at where my life began, I am so grateful for whatever the universe has given me and my family. My life started with the partition of India. From those hardships to the beginning of my career as a stenographer and then a sales manager - the struggles were enormous and sometimes felt never ending. Even after we began Sonarome, the struggles we saw because of minimal financial resources and a rigid and unfriendly banking system were daunting. I am grateful that we sailed through without losing our sanity. We worked hard and long and built a world-class company.

At this stage in life, I have incurred many personal losses. The passing away of my closest friends, Bhagwandass Gandhi, Naveen and Lulu Patel, Ajit Lamba, Sarabjit Bajaj, Sunil Thakurdas, Sethi and a few others, have left me feeling alone. I miss them often and realize that I too am in the queue. My father used to say that you are living if your efforts are remembered by others. Thus, our efforts should always focus on doing good for others, especially the poor and the needy.

I admire and thank my wife, Ramandeep, who has always been the source of strength during those difficult times. Even though she is younger than me by a few years, I have learned a lot from her. We are proud of our children. I wish that she lives many more years and continues to hold my hand in both good and bad times.

Today, we have money in the bank, comfortable homes for us and each of the children, financial freedom, and still the gift of good health. My eyes look to the sky, and I raise my hands in prayer.

Thank you, Waheguru, for all your blessings, especially the strength you provided to work *"Against All Odds."*

Whatever happens in the future, in our remaining time on this earth, will be, God willing, good.

ABOUT THE AUTHOR

Mr. Trilok Singh Gulhati was born in Mardan (North-West Frontier Province- now in Pakistan) in 1938. He began his professional journey as a stenographer, and then moved on to become a salesman for Hindustan Unilever, and eventually ascended the ranks to become the Regional Manager at Gabriel India, followed by a stint at Siemens, India. Soon after, he was appointed as the National Sales Manager at Warner-Lambert and was responsible for launching two popular products, Chiclets, and Halls Mentholyptus, into the Indian market.

He then moved to Reckitt & Colman and made the successful launch of Disprin possible.

Mr. Gulhati began his entrepreneurial journey when he founded Sonarome, now India's leading company in flavors and fragrances. He has taught marketing at Bhavan's College, lectured at Staff Collect Hyderabad, and was also a visiting faculty at IIM Bangalore.

Sonarome started in a humble shed in the Peenya Industrial Area and has since grown to occupy a sprawling 6-acre campus with state-of-the-art manufacturing, application, quality control, and research and development laboratories.

Sonarome is rated as the top Indian F&F company, selling its products to over 4,000 businesses in India and 45 countries across the globe. Mr. Gulhati, the head of Sonarome Private Limited, leads a team of more than 150 happy employees. His reputation in the flavors and fragrance industry is unmatched.

Mr. Gulhati passed away on 15ᵗʰ July 2023.

www.ingramcontent.com/pod-product-compliance
Lightning Source LLC
Chambersburg PA
CBHW030501100426
42813CB00002B/304

.